To Bobby—
My First and Best Pet

Endpapers by M. Gilroy.

A Beginner's Guide to
Hamsters

Written by
Jay Stephens

Contents

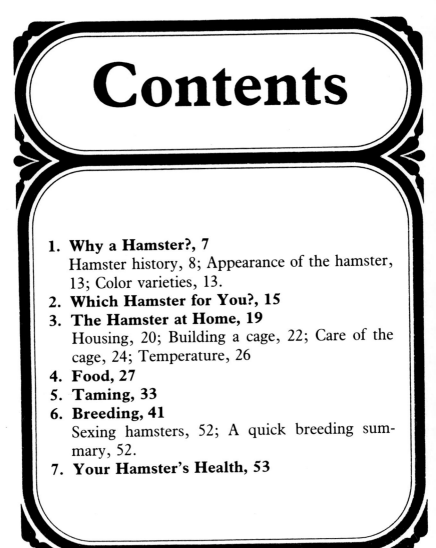

1.
Why a Hamster?

So you are seriously considering a hamster for a pet? Or perhaps you have just acquired your first one. In either case you undoubtedly have a slew of questions to be answered, and it is the purpose of this small book to try to answer them. It was written not to be scientific and scholarly but to be informative and easily understood

An adult golden hamster and part of her litter.

by every man, woman, boy or girl who wants to know how to care properly for his or her new pet and, in so doing, thoroughly enjoy it.

It is hard to think of any pet more enjoyable to keep or easier to maintain than the hamster, and particularly so if you live in the city. Here's why: he is inexpensive to purchase, his cage takes up little room. He is easy to feed and care for. He requires no grooming. He is a healthy animal without any odor of his own.

And to top it all, once tamed, this funny little ball of fur no bigger than your hand turns into a delightfully amusing companion who likes nothing better in this world than to be petted.

The first question almost always asked is: just what is a hamster? The hamster is a charming little animal with a twinkling little face and alert black eyes, belonging to the rodent family. He looks some say, like a tiny bear; and others, a field mouse or chipmunk. That he resembles a cross between a large mouse and a small guinea pig is the closest comparison. When fully grown, the Golden Hamster is about six inches long with ony a tiny stub of a tail. He is now bred in varying shades but his natural color is red-gold. His most amazing and characteristic feature, is however, his cheek pouches which swell up like balloons when he uses them to store away uneaten food.

Most people start out with only a single hamster. Many soon acquire breeding pairs or trios—one male and two females, and before long have dozens of animals. You can stick to one or have dozens. The number isn't nearly as important as the fun you'll have, the knowledge that you will acquire, and the enjoyment that you will receive from the hobby of keeping and training hamsters.

Hamster history

The hamster's name tells us a lot about this friendly fellow's favorite habit—hoarding. *Hamster* in German means hoarder. Your hamster, as have thousands of ancestors before him, loves to stuff his cheek pouches with food and then run away to store his treasures for a rainy day. So startling is it to see a hamster's head swell up into balloon size that many new owners upon seeing it for the first time have phoned the veterinarian to tell him their pet has mumps!

8   *Hamsters are among the most desirable of small pets. Photo by M. Gilroy.*

A young cream banded hamster with its cream littermates.
Photo by M. Gilroy.

Hamsters now come in a bewildering variety of colors a
coat textures. Although most of these newer varieties are s
almost unobtainable and quite expensive, there is still h
that they will eventually become common and afforda
Photo by M. Gil

A black-eyed white hamster, one of the newest strains. Note the prominent cheek pouches in this specimen. Photo by M. Gilroy.

Although Golden Hamsters were introduced into this country in 1938 as laboratory animals they did not take the pet world by storm until 1947. Today there are untold millions of them in the United States alone.

And it all began in 1930 with one mother and twelve young hamsters which a zoologist found in the Syrian desert which is situated in the Middle East to the north of Israel. Deep in a burrow eight feet underground he came upon a hamster mother and her litter. But by the time he got his tiny family back to his laboratory in Jerusalem, all but three of them had died or escaped. These three, however, continued in excellent health and within four months the first litter of Golden Hamsters ever to be born in captivity was delivered.

As they matured, these babies were interbred, and as the tame hamsters multiplied they were used in research experiments. Soon they began to attract widespread attention in the scientific world. Because hamsters were so disease-free and bred so rapidly—they can have a new litter every month!—and because they were so friendly and easy to handle, they came to be highly regarded as laboratory animals and their fame spread throughout the world accordingly.

From Jerusalem scientists took them to laboratories in France, England and, in 1938, to the United States. All present-day Golden Hamsters in captivity, with the exception of a few brought back by travelers and military men, are the descendants of that first tiny family found in Syria.

For the scientifically minded, the Golden Hamster's correct name is *Mesocricetus auratus*, usually shortened to *M. auratus*. It is also referred to as the Syrian Golden Hamster. In Syria and other Middle Eastern countries where hamsters are common, the farmers harvest not only their own fields, but they dig into the hamster's granaries as well. In each burrow they find a storage bin which may hold anywhere between 30 and 60 pounds of grain which the hamsters have stored away for the winter.

Appearance of the hamster

In appearance, many people think the Golden Hamster resembles a tiny bear, and it is easy to see why when you see a hamster standing on his back legs. He is red-gold in color, with the underside of his body a grayish white, and with black markings on his head and cheeks. His eyes are black. He is between five and six inches long when mature with a stub of a tail and expandable cheek pouches.

Color varieties: These are becoming more and more common as a result of mutations turning up and the selective breeding of mutants. Among the following are the color varieties most commonly encountered:
Albino—White fur, pink eyes, dark ears.*Panda or Piebald*—Golden with white spotting.*Amber-gold or Cinnamon*—Amber or fawn-colored fur. Claret eyes; light-colored ears.*Cream*—Light cream fur, black ears and eyes.*White Band*—Similar to original Golden but with a one-inch white band running around its midriff.

The Albinos sometimes suffer from defective vision. This is because their pink eyes are highly sensitive to light. None of the hamsters, however, have very good vision because they are all nocturnal animals: they prefer to sleep all day and prowl at night.

A female golden dominant spot hamster. Actually, this looks much like an everyday hamster. Photo by M. Gilroy.

2.
Which Hamster for you?

When buying a hamster (or any other pet for that matter) it is always wise to go to a reputable pet shop or breeder. Don't try for a bargain. Good hamsters are not that expensive.

Back view of a shy dwarf hamster,
Podopus sungorus, *from Russia.*

Look for a hamster between five and eight weeks old. Baby hamsters are easily frightened so it is useless to attempt to tame one until he's a little, but not much, older. It is also wise to remember that a hamster's natural life-span is only about two years, so get one when he's young and you'll have that much longer to enjoy him.

Pet shops vary in the way they maintain and display their hamsters. Keeping them in individual cages is undoubtedly the best way but many shops do not do this because they haven't enough space. It is best not to choose a hamster from a community cage containing both sexes of unknown age. You may end up with a pregnant female.

Take your time. Ask the dealer to show you as many animals as you care to examine. You'll want to make sure that the one of your choice is in excellent physical condition with an even disposition. First look for all-round signs of friendliness and good health—soft sleek fur, clear bright eyes, and a feel of solidity. Avoid bony animals. A good hamster feels solid to the heft.

A black-eyed cream hamster.

Do not purchase hamsters less than five to eight weeks old; these little black-eyed creams would still be too young for adoption. Photo by M. Gilroy.

Examine the ears. They give a good idea of the hamster's age. In a young animal the insides of the ears are covered with tiny white hairs; these gradually disappear with age and in the older animal the ears are hairless and shiny.

Look at the nose, feet and belly. There should be no pimples or other blemishes. These are signs of mange. If you find an animal with a runny nose or watery eyes, or one whose movements are lethargic, avoid him too. A wet tail is also a sign of bad health. Make sure there are no scars or bald patches in his pelt.

You may, however, accept small spots on the hips. They are called dimorphic pigment spots and are perfectly normal. They are more prominent in the male than the female.

Some hamsters have nicks in their ears. These are usually the breeder's marks, used by him as cattlemen use brands. They have no ill effects.

How many should you buy? This, of course, is up to you. Do you want to breed hamsters or do you want to keep just one as a pet? If the latter, no need to feel sorry for it because it's lonely. In their natural state, hamsters live by themselves except in mating season. If yours gets a reasonable amount of attention he will be quite content to live alone and be the center of attraction.

If you do want more than one hamster, remember that after they are mature they cannot be kept in the same cage. Several males from the same litter can sometimes live happily together but females, once they are of breeding age, rarely can.

Male or female? Sex isn't too important if you decide on only one animal. The females have a tendency as they grow older to become less friendly; the males almost always remain docile. If you do select a female, check her carefully to make sure that she is not already pregnant—unless, of course, you want to start off with a ready-made family. Ask the dealer to determine this for you. Of course, if she is nearly ready to litter, her condition will be obvious.

If you do decide to start out with a pair, it is better to choose them from different bloodlines. Brother and sister matings are not desirable.

Don't choose your hamster just from observing him in his cage. Ask the dealer to take him out and place him on a table or the counter. Do not, of course, try to take the hamster from the cage yourself. Observe the seller carefully while he does this. Is he nervous and squeamish about putting his hand in the cage? It may be because the hamster isn't too tame.

Even after the hamster has been placed on the table, do not try to pick him up. Tempt him with a grain of corn, a sunflower seed, or peanut. Chances are he'll take it from your hand. Remember that he is very nervous so don't make any sudden moves.

If the hamster does not scurry away from your outstretched hand, let him see the back of it for a moment, then close it gently around his entire body so that he is cradled in your fist. Never swoop down on a hamster from above. Always let him see your hand coming. Some owners like to pick up their pets by bringing their hands together on either side of him and scooping him up in their palms. Be very careful that he doesn't fall. Hamsters do not land on their feet like cats. A fall can prove fatal.

When you have picked him up successfully, examine him with the points in mind that we have just outlined. If he is difficult to pick up, seems afraid or tries to bite, select another animal and repeat the procedure.

3.
The Hamster at home

Your hamster will not require a great deal of maintenance. But the few things he does require are essential, and great pains should be taken to see that he gets them.

Tortoiseshell hamsters. Photo by M. Gilroy.

Housing

There are many types of cages available in pet shops and variety stores designed especially for hamsters. Some are elaborate and expensive; others are smaller, simpler, and more reasonable in price. Your pocketbook will have to be your guide here unless you have the skill to build your own.

The most convenient of the commercial hamster cages are those made of metal and resembling a bird cage. They are equipped with a bottom which slides in and out facilitating their cleaning. As we have said, they come in various sizes; buy the largest you can afford. The hamster is an active animal who likes to climb around. He may become nervous and snappish if kept too long in a cage that is too small.

A rule of thumb is a square foot of space for each hamster. A cage that is two feet long, eighteen inches deep and a foot high is preferable.

The bottom should be padded or lined with one or two inches of a good absorbent material, You can use wood shavings, a commercially prepared hamster litter, or even thicknesses of newspaper. Cedar shavings are perhaps the best, but many hamsters prefer newspaper; they enjoy shredding it. However, paper does not absorb as efficiently as do many other materials.

Never use old blanket material or any fabric to line a hamster's cage. He will chew and swallow it, upsetting his digestion. Moreover, fabric quickly becomes wet and dirty, and it is not so easy to dispose of as commercially prepared litter, newspaper, or wood shavings. Avoid any bedding material which might irritate or lacerate the cheek pouches.

Next you will need a feeding dish and a hamster water dispenser. The feeding dish need not be too large, but it should be securely fastened to the side of the cage so that it cannot be knocked over. It should be accessible from outside the cage so that it will not be necessary to open it every time you want to feed your pet.

The water dispenser is necessary because the hamsters will quickly make a mess of their cage if water is given to them in an open dish. Such a water dispenser can be bought inexpensively at pet shops or

Every hamster needs a home. Photo by M. Gilroy.

you can make your own by taking a small bottle and fitting it with a rubber cork (obtainable at drug or hardware stores). Fill the bottle, plug the cork in tightly, and hang it upside down on the outside of the cage with the curved tip penetrating inside. Drops of water will form at the tip of the tube and continue to form, one by one, as the hamster licks them off. Always make sure that even the baby hamsters can reach the tip of the tube.

To make sure that your pet gets plenty of exercise, try to find a cage equipped with a wire exercise wheel. If not, buy a wheel and install it yourself. Another fun and exercise device is a little slide. Hamsters love to play with these devices and the exercise is good for them.

Building a cage: If you decide to build you own cage, there are several things to keep in mind. For one, the hamster is a gnawing animal and he will gnaw through a wooden cage unless it is strongly reinforced with hardware cloth or wire netting. Use at least 5/8-inch *hardwood* for the floor, back and sides of the cage, and wire mesh for the front and top.

The cage should be approximately 24 inches long, 12 inches high, 18 inches from front to back. A hinged trapdoor can be cut into one of the ends or, if preferred, the entire mesh-covered top can be a hinged lid with a catch to keep it closed.

Paint the entire inside with a non-toxic enamel; this helps to discourage gnawing. The outside, of course, can be painted any attractive color you prefer.

The wooden floor must be lined with metal. This not only ensures that the hamster cannot gnaw his way out; it makes the floor that much easier to keep clean. A flat metal pan, like a cookie sheet, can be used for this purpose; it can be cut to size and easily slid in and out for cage cleaning. Such a metal bottom will prevent droppings and stored food and urine from penetrating the bottom of the cage to cause odor.

A separate sleeping chamber or nest not less than six inches square should be placed inside the cage. This too should be of metal with a removable top to make cleaning easier. If you do not give your hamster such a little nest (and some owners do not because the

A female light gray long-haired hamster. Photo by M. Gilroy.

Exercise is vital to the happiness of your hamster. He will do lots of running around at night and needs things to play with.

hamster spends too much time in it) make sure he has plenty of straw, shavings, excelsior, etc., to hide in whenever he feels like it.

When selecting a spot in which to keep the cage, choose one that is warm and free of drafts and out of the sunlight. It should be in a room with a relatively constant temperature. A sudden drop of temperature can cause a hamster to go into hibernation. Remember too that he is a nocturnal animal. Given his choice he will sleep all day and begin his activities when the sun goes down. Because of this, his cage should be kept in a dark corner.

Care of the cage: The hamster's cage should be cleaned thoroughly at least once a week; oftener if the litter becomes damp. One of the all-purpose cleaners with a pine scent is good for this. It will help keep down odors. Then wipe with a creosol disinfectant.

When you clean the cage, you will find stored-away food. Remove some, especially if it is decaying, but not all because this will upset the hamster and he will spend much time searching for it. Replace the rest in the spot you found it.

A male cream long-haired hamster. Photo by M. Gilroy.

This is true too of the little wads of bedding you will discover. Restore them after cleaning. The hamster doesn't like having to make his bed any more than you do and he will be greatly annoyed if he has to start all over again.

The hamster's droppings are pellet-like and firm. A corner of the cage as far from the nest as possible will be used for urination. This corner should be cleaned out every day and replaced with new litter. Some owners solve this problem by using a jar with a wide mouth big enough for the hamster to enter. They place this jar on its side in the corner of the cage which the hamster himself has chosen for his toilet. He will use this jar, and the floor of the cage will remain dry. The jar, of course, should be washed out daily and replaced when it becomes stained.

Make sure that his feeding dish is kept scrupulously clean, and that the water bottle is refilled each day, and the tube flushed out with running water.

Temperature: Hamsters should be kept in a room with a temperature between 55 and 70°F. Older hamsters can stand lower temperatures but the newborn cannot. A drop of temperature to 45°F may cause him to go into a state of hibernation. He will sleep, the body will become rigid, and his temperature will fall below normal. If this should happen to your hamster do not make the mistake that some novice owners have made: destroying their pet thinking he was dead. Slow, gentle warming with *your* body heat will usually "thaw" him out.

4.

Food

Your hamster's diet is basically a simple one. He will need hard grains like wheat or corn, seeds like sunflower seeds, and occasionally fresh greens and fruit. He loves vegetables of the root type, carrots especially, and likes to have his menu varied. Grains and seeds

Hamsters love carrots and other root vegetables. Photo by H. Lacey.

are the mainstay of his diet and this is as it should be because they help him to grind down his teeth. Perishable foods like green vegetables and fruit are necessary too but they should not be fed too often because they can cause mildew on the cage floor and diarrhea in the hamster.

Commercially prepared hamster food is available at most pet shops and it will supply the vitamins and minerals that your pet requires. About a tablespoonful a day should be enough; a box will last about a month.

Avoid as much as possible foods containing a high percentage of water. Avoid too much milk as well. While milk is very good for hamsters, contributing greatly to their growth and maintaining their teeth in good condition, it is dangerous when it begins to turn sour. The writer feeds his hamsters dry milk, making sure that no moisture touches it.

The chief reason for feeding only dry food is the hamster's habit of storing all food away. Foods with a high moisture content decay quickly and develop harmful bacteria.

If regular hamster chow is not available, or if you run short, you may substitute chicken feed, kibbled dog or cat food, bird seed, dry bread, or breakfast cereal temporarily, but you should return to the prepared food as soon as possible. Pamper your pet at times by giving him a treat of sunflower seeds, peanuts, or raisins. It will make taming and training that much easier because if he enjoys these treats they can be used as rewards.

Because it is so amusing to watch a hamster stuff his cheek pouches this leads to the temptation to feed him often. No harm in this. No matter how much food you supply him with, he will not overeat. He enjoys storing away excess food.

Since the hamster is most active in the early evening, this is the best time to feed him. It is better to establish a regular feeding time and stick to it. In this way he learns that he is to be fed at a certain time and comes to expect it. One feeding a day is enough.

One of the advantages of owning a hamster is that he can take care of himself if you are going to be away a few days. Make sure his water bottle is filled (if necessary give him two bottles) and give

Head view of a dwarf hamster. So far these all have the same color pattern of a blackish stripe on the back and a shaggy grayish look. Photo by M. Gilroy.

him a large supply of dry food. He'll get along fine for about a week.

The hamster does not require much water but his water-bottle should be freshly filled each day.

If you have to move his feed dish return it to the same spot. Hamsters are creatures of habit.

Hamsters like live food too. They have been known to eat ants, sow bugs, cockroaches, flies, even hornets. So if you have any of these available feed them to him occasionally—live if possible.

Fresh fruit and vegetables should always be washed thoroughly before being offered. They have been sprayed with insecticides which are harmful to hamsters. Nor should more fresh food than can be consumed in a day be fed. Spoiled food or soured milk can result in intestinal disturbances.

A few *don'ts* concerning hamster feeding: they should not be fed any of the acid fruits like oranges or grapefruit although orange peels are enjoyed. Nor should they be given the needles of evergreen trees, either as food or bedding. Raw meat should be avoided too. It seems to encourage cannibalism. Garlic they don't like and onions will make them furious.

A satin cinnamon female hamster. Satin refers to a type of glossy coat texture. Photo by M. Gilroy.

Hamsters are seed-eaters in nature, so they will seldom turn down seeds of any type, especially when made nice and nibbly as a treat. Photo by Dr. Herbert R. Axelrod.

5.
Taming

A new hamster is a nervous hamster. Make things easy for yours when you first bring him home. Make doubly sure that no one frightens him with sudden movements or loud talk. Avoid starting

Ladder-climbing is a trick easily taught to any hamster.

The first step in training your hamster is to teach it to enjoy gentle handling.

up any noisy electrical appliance in his presence. It is wiser to let him alone for the first few days until he shows without prompting his desire to be friendly.

If your hamster arrives in a box, open it carefully. You will probably find him burrowed down in the bedding. Do not thrust you hand in suddenly. He is more than likely to nip it. Let him first see the back of your hand. Then slip it firmly around his shoulders so that the head lies in the palm, facing the wrist. Quickly put him in his cage, which of course you have already prepared according to the instructions given under "HOUSING".

Make sure that his water-bottle and food cup are full and leave him alone, observing him, if at all, from a distance, remembering always that hamsters have sensitive nervous systems and that strange noises and voices will only terrify them.

Only when your new hamster has accepted his surroundings and set up housekeeping, so to speak, should you attempt to become acquainted. He will make his bed, establish his pantry, and choose a corner for his "bathroom". The female is usually more fussy about this than the male. He is inclined to be lazy.

Taming is a simple procedure. It is chiefly a matter of gaining your pet's confidence. He is, by nature, a gentle, friendly fellow and you, too, must be gentle, friendly—and patient! Patience is particularly important.

First put your hand into his cage slowly. Offer him a tidbit like a sunflower seed, a peanut or a raisin, holding it in the palm of your hand. Although he may seem shy at first, his natural curiosity will finally overcome his nervousness, and he will come over to investigate and start nibbling. Now try stroking him gently. When you sense that he is friendly enough to be picked up, do it in the manner just described. Lift him out of the cage and place him on a table. Watch him closely, however, because hamsters have poor vision and yours might walk right off the edge. A hamster is not able to turn his body in mid-air like a cat can, so such a fall can sometimes prove fatal. Pet him now and talk to him softly, using his name—yes, hamsters learn the sound of their name.

Do this as often as possible until your hamster gets completely used to you. The next step is to place your hand and arm on the table

This golden umbrous satin angora hamster enjoys toys. Even pure-breds can have fun! Photo by M. Gilroy.

Once tamed, a hamster will enjoy being picked up and handled. His strong feet prevent him from falling easily, but be careful anyway.

so that he can climb up it and into your pockets or onto your shoulders. Don't worry now that he will fall. Hamster feet are well adapted to climbing and he is in no danger unless you make a sudden startled movement.

Next, unless you have a dog or cat, you can put your hamster on the floor and allow him to wander around. Keep a close eye on him, however. Remember an adult hamster can crawl through a hole the size of a quarter, and a baby hamster through one the size of a dime; so you may have trouble finding him again, especially if he gets under the floor. Remember too that hamsters like to gnaw, so keep an eye on the furniture.

Once your hamster has become completely tamed, you can start teaching him tricks. Having a pet that can perform will be a never-ending source of pleasure as well as pride.

Patience, perseverance and repetition are the keys to success. How well you are able to train your hamster depends on how well you

A black-eyed white female hamster. Photo by M. Gilroy.

apply these three keys and on how much imagination you can bring to the training process.

The use of a reward is extremely important. This should be a treat that you know your hamster enjoys. Hold it high above his head so that he will have to stand on his hind legs to reach it. Repeat his name and the command "Stand" until he does, make him "waltz" for a moment and then give him his reward. Repeat this procedure and the command again and again until he stands whenever you hold your hand over his head, even without the reward. He will soon come to associate the word "Stand" with the act of standing, and do so whenever ordered.

Other commands can be taught in the same way, always remembering to repeat the identical word and procedure. By this same method you can teach him his name. Hold a bit of food out to him and call him by name. He will come for the food, but after constantly hearing his name repeated he will come to realize that that means him.

Treats are essential in training a hamster. For the right treat a hamster will eve come when called.

A fawn female hamster. Photo by M. Gilroy.

There are no short cuts to training. As we have just said, patience and perseverance are the keys. If you fail at first, don't say "My hamster's too dumb to learn" but keep on trying until you succeed. Be gentle, keep your voice calm and even, and don't give up. It may take time but the result will be worth it.

Hamsters love to play and if you implement this natural playfulness with a playground you will find yourself spending many happy hours watching their amusing antics.

There are a great many toys on the market especially designed for hamsters. Parakeet toys are good for them too. We have already mentioned the exercise wheel. Most new hamster cages come equipped with these wheels, but if yours did not, or you have built your own cage, buy a wheel at your pet shop. They are not expensive and homemade ones require a certain amount of skill. If the cage is large enough, you may keep the wheel set up permanently; if not, set it up outside for your hamster's daily exercise period.

It is natural for hamsters to dig, and happy the hamster who has a sandbox of his own. This need be no more than a wooden grocery box filled about a foot deep with sand. Surround the box with a sea of newspaper and let your hamster burrow to his heart's content. Under supervision, of course. Make sure he cannot escape.

6.
Breeding

Until hamsters were first domesticated in 1930, it was assumed that rats and mice had the shortest period of pregnancy of any mammal—21 days. But the female hamster breaks that record easily with her gestation period of 16 days. She can have her first litter

A mother hamster and her two-week-old babies.

when she is only eight weeks old and then, if birth control is non-existent, continue to have a litter almost every month for the rest of the year, with an average of seven babies each time. In that same year, her children, grandchildren, great grandchildren, *ad libitum*, will start having litters. So within twelve months (and providentially, female hamsters produce fewer young after that first year) one pair of hamsters can, theoretically, generate one hundred thousand decendants!

Although the average hamster is capable of breeding when it is eight weeks old it is wiser to wait until the female is about three months old before mating her for the first time. She will be better able to stand the strain.

The female's estrus cycle (period of sexual heat) repeats itself every four days, but she can only be impregnated during the night of the first day. Since it is difficult for the novice to tell just which day this is, the simplest procedure is to place the female in the male's cage for a period of no more than a week. This, however, is not quite as easy as it sounds. Many females, if they are not ready for mating, will fight the male viciously so a careful introduction is necessary.

A litter of cinnamon hamsters about ten days old. They grow fast!
Photo by M. Gilroy.

Baby black hamsters about 12 days old. Photo by M. Gilroy.

A male hamster. Notice the bulging rear profile. Photo by Hanson.

A female hamster. Notice the blunter rear profile. Photo by M. F. Roberts.

Close-up of a two-week-old hamster. The eyes are not yet open though the fur is growing well.

Solid color hamsters are becoming more popular. Photo by M. Gilroy.

Twenty-day-old hamsters. The eyes are open and the fur is thick and like mother's. Photo by M. Gilroy.

Never, but never, put the male into the female's cage. This is her home and she will defend it. When you have selected your breeding pair (and for a strong healthy litter they should come from different bloodlines, not be brother and sister), switch the male to the female's cage and the female to the male's cage—separated, of course, until they get used to each other's cage-scent. Next return them to their own cages, but place the cages side by side so that they can get acquainted through the bars. Only now, if they seem compatible, should the female be introduced into the male's cage, and it is wise to wear gloves when you do it, because there may be a fight and you should be ready to control it. If the female is *not* in heat, such a fight is almost certain. The only time she will show affection is when she is ready to mate.

If she is ready, she will probably go rigid, tail up, head held low. Both animals will start running around the cage with occasional halts to inspect each other. When the female decides to accept the male she will crouch and await his attentions.

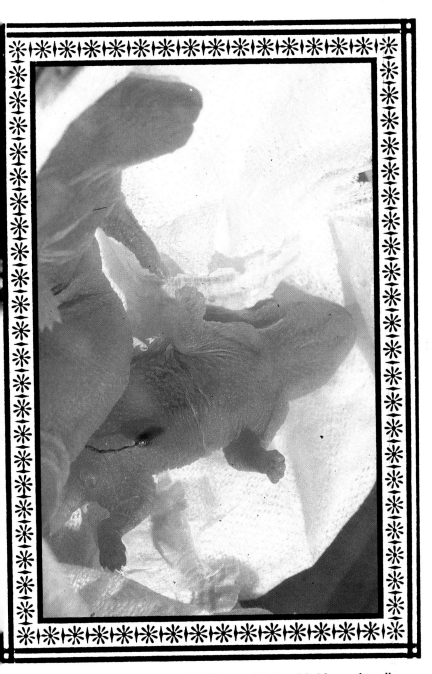

Baby hamsters less than an hour old. They are blind and hairless and totally helpless. Photo by M. Gilroy.

But if a fight ensues, return the female to her cage and try again the next day. Some breeders claim that a young female finds an older male more compatible.

This introduction should be made at night. Being nocturnal animals, hamsters prefer to do their mating then.

If on the first meeting no mating occurs but the hamsters accept each other peacefully, it is safe to leave them together in the same cage for as much as a week; at the end of that week, if you are not certain whether mating has taken place, remove the female to her litter-cage anyway and wait to see if she shows signs of pregnancy. If two weeks go by without anything happening you will know that the mating was unsuccessful. Try again.

Before the female is returned to her litter-cage a nest box should be provided. This should be about six inches square with an opening just big enough for a pregnant female to squeeze through. Excelsior, straw, hay or shredded paper should be provided for nesting material, but this should be placed in the outer cage. She will want to build her own nest. Do not even look into this nest until nine days after the litter is born.

During her entire pregnancy she should be left alone as much as possible. Keep cage cleaning to a minimum. Add milk to her diet (preferably powdered), see that she gets more green vegetables and, of course, fresh water. This added diet should continue until she has weaned her young.

The young are born usually at night. You can anticipate it if you know the exact time of mating. It will be exactly 16 days, give or take a few hours, later. The newborn hamsters (which you probably won't see because they are in the nest and it is inadvisable to look in) are about an inch long and weigh less than an eighth of an ounce. There can be any number from one to a dozen but the average is seven. The babies are born naked and blind but they need no care and should be left entirely to their mother.

Warning: Don't even touch one except in an emergency. The mother, resenting the new smell from your hand, is more than likely to destroy the baby. If for any reason you do have to touch a nursling, handle all in the litter so they will smell the same.

A male cinnamon banded satin hamster. Photo by Hanson.

For the first nine days after birth, the little family should be left completely alone except for feeding or, if necessary, the removal of a dead animal. Only then should regular cage cleaning be resumed.

When they are about eight days old, the baby hamsters will start wandering around the cage, going to the toilet and eating the solid food which their mother will offer them. Their eyes, however, will still be closed, not to open for 14 days. Once they do start eating solid food, be sure to increase the daily rations.

When hamsters are about five weeks old—they will have been weaned in 21 days—they should be separated according to sex to prevent premature breeding, but each sex can be kept in a community cage until they begin to fight among themselves. That means they too are now ready for breeding.

Sexing Hamsters

Hold the animal in the palm of your hand on its back. The penis of the male is about 1/4 to 1/2 inch from the vent. The vulva of the female is closer to the vent and is mostly bare except for a few grayish hairs. The general body contour is also an aid. The male presents a tapered, elongated rear, while the rear of the female is more blunt and not as brightly colored as that of the male.

A quick breeding summary

Period. Will breed throughout year; most litters between May and November.
First Possible Mating: At 43 days.
First Possible Litter: 59 days; average 73 days.
Mating Time: Introduce female to male after 6:30 p.m. Mating is immediate if female is in heat.
Estrus Cycle: Repeats every four days: impregnation possible only on night of first day.
Gestation Period: 16 days.
Number of Young in Litter: 1 to 15; average 7.
First Solid Food: 8 days.
Eyes Open: 14-15 days.
Weaning: 18-21 days.
Caging: Separate young males from females at 35 days.

7.

Hamster's health

A clean dry cage is essential to your hamster's health. He does not like dampness; he will suffer from it. Do not let the bedding litter become saturated with urine.

Healthy hamsters have a bright-eyed look that is unmistakable.

A patterned yellow hamster. Photo by M. Gilroy.

Never allow uneaten pieces of fruit to accumulate in the cage. This can lead to invasions by insect pests.

Do not put water or milk in a cup for drinking purposes. It is almost certain to be spilled into the bedding. Do not leave uneaten fruits or vegetables to accumulate in the cage. If bedding does become wet, replace it immediately.

Be sure that wild rats or mice do not have access to your hamster's cage. They are disease carriers. If you purchase a new hamster make sure that he is in good health before you bring him into the same room with the others.

When using an insecticide on household pests like ants, roaches or bugs, remove the hamster to another room when spraying.

When you have cleaned and disinfected the hamster's cage, never return him to it until the cage is bone-dry.

Hamsters are rarely attacked by mites or fleas, but if this should happen, commercial sprays are available. If not, use a bird mite

Female cream hamsters. Photo by M. Gilroy.

*Facing page: Stuffed cheek pouches are typical
of healthy hamsters.*

spray. Do not use any spray or medication prepared for dogs on hamsters. Cat preparations are okay.

Hamsters are susceptible to human colds and respiratory infections. So if any member of the family is suffering from a cold, bar him from the hamster room or isolate the hamster. A widemouthed glass jar with litter on the bottom and wire mesh taped across the top can serve as a temporary home. If your hamster does catch cold make sure that his cage is in a warm, dry place and cover it with newspapers or heavy fabric to keep out drafts. Allow for ventilation. Give him a little cod-liver oil: a few drops on a piece of bread is enough. Clean out all old litter and replace with fresh. Do this again after he has recovered.

The best way to tell if something is wrong with your hamster is to compare his present behavior with normal behavior. A healthy animal upon wakening (and do not expect this liveliness during the bright hours of day) will run around his cage, wash himself, stand on his hind legs, and climb around his cage. His fur will be clean and smooth and he will carry his stubby tail erect. Listlessness, dull

Any unusual behavior by your hamster may the sign of illness, so be sure to pay close attention to it at least a few minutes every day. Photo by M. Gilroy.

Flesh-eared albino hamsters, one long-haired, the other normal. These are true albinos. Photo by Hanson.

eyes, no appetite, ruffled coat, and general emaciation are all negative indications.

The hamster's teeth are probably his greatest weakness. They break off, acquire cavities, and are subject to decay. Teeth broken from falls or biting wire can result in an inability to eat. If this happens, adjacent teeth should be clipped with heavy duty nail clippers so that they mesh easily with broken teeth enabling the animal to eat.

Many times a hamster's dental problems can be solved by adding more milk to his diet. This can be fed instead of water in his dispenser, or by feeding bread and milk, or (and preferably) by using dry milk. Care must be taken that the milk does not sour and that milk-soaked bread is not hoarded.

As to wounds or cuts, there is no need to be concerned about them if the hamster can reach them with his tongue; his constant licking will prevent their becoming infected. Otherwise, treat them with a mild antiseptic, like tincture of merthiolate applied with a cotton swab. Do not bandage the wound. If it is bleeding freely hold a bit of gauze against it firmly until the blood clots. A wounded hamster should never be kept in a cage with others. They are likely to attack him.

The hamster's droppings are a good clue to his health. If they are pellet-shaped and of firm consistency all is well. Loose watery droppings indicate too much fresh fruit and vegetables; hard dry droppings indicate not enough. Constipation is more common among young hamsters; make sure that they get plenty of fresh water.

Another disability related to improper diet is Cage Paralysis. The hamster cannot raise his head and moves along pushing his nose on the floor. This results from a lack of Vitamin D and not enough exercise. Cod-liver oil will supply the needed vitamin.

Since the hamster is such a remarkable healthy animal, chances are that you will not be faced with any of the above ailments. If something does appear seriously wrong and you are unable to handle it with any of these suggestions, isolate the hamster at once and consult your veterinarian. A really diseased animal will, perhaps, have to be destroyed.

Although they have been pets less than 50 years, hamsters have become standard first pets for many children. Photo by M. Gilroy.